THE PHOTOGRAPHIC HERITAGE
OF THE MIDDLE EAST

*An Exhibition of Early Photographs
of Egypt, Palestine, Syria, Turkey,
Greece, & Iran, 1849-1893*

ℬ *by Paul E. Chevedden*

UNDENA PUBLICATIONS, MALIBU

Exhibited at the Department of Special Collections,
UCLA Research Library
November 5, 1981 - February 21, 1982

This catalog was made possible in part by assistance from
the Gustave E. von Grunebaum Center
for Near Eastern Studies, UCLA

ISBN: 0-89003-096-0
© 1981 by Paul E. Chevedden

UNDENA PUBLICATIONS
P. O. Box 97, Malibu, CA. 90265

PREFACE

This exhibition of early photographs of the Middle East grew out of conversations with the UCLA Library's Near Eastern Bibliographer, Dunning Wilson. Through my own dissertation research on the city wall and fortifications of Damascus, I had become familiar with many collections of early photography of the Middle East, but I was unaware of the significant collection at UCLA until Dunning informed me of it in the fall of 1980 upon my return to the United States. We decided that this collection should be put on public view not only to show the Middle East as it was recorded over a century ago by the first photographers, but also to demonstrate the importance of this region in the history of photography. During the early decades of photography no other area of the world excepting Europe, was so thoroughly photographed as was the Middle East, particularly Egypt and Palestine. The earliest photographic processes were employed in the Middle East almost immediately after they were developed in Europe; some of the first books to be illustrated with original photographs dealt with regions of this area; and the first application of photography as a documentary tool of scientific exploration took place in the Middle East when the early daguerreotypists recorded hieroglyphs on Egyptian temples. The prominence the Middle East holds in the development and diffusion of the photographic industry is a well established fact, yet there are still numerous gaps in our knowledge of the early photographers who worked there; the history of their labors can only be traced in broad detail. It is hoped that the exhibition will encourage further research into this subject and foster greater public awareness of the early photography of the Middle East.

This exhibition and catalog benefited from the efforts of many individuals. I am most grateful to Dunning Wilson for his encouragement and help throughout the entire course of this project and to my mother for laboring over the typescript and contending with many revisions. I would like to acknowledge with thanks the following for providing me with pertinent information which was incorporated into the catalog: Bernard Marbot, Conservateur, Photographie Ancienne, Département des Estampes et de la Photographie, Bibliothèque Nationale; Beaumont Newhall; Pierre Apraxine, curator of the Gilman Paper Company Collection; Ingeborg O'Reilly, photo-archivist at the Harvard Semitic Museum; and Stanford J. Shaw and Claude Audebert of UCLA. Ruth Gibbs, Associate University Librarian, and her assistant, James Davis, generously read and improved the text of the catalog and gave great support to the exhibition. Marie Louise Penchoen and Ann West of Undena Publications prepared the catalog for production. I thank them for their considerable efforts under the pressure of a tight schedule. The Department of Special Collections helped organize the exhibition and thanks are due to its entire staff, particularly Brooke Whiting, Hilda Bohem, Pearl Rosenfeld, Jeffrey Rankin, and most especially, Lilace Hatayama. I am most grateful to Marian Engelke of the UCLA Library Printing Office who designed the captions and mounted the photographs for the exhibition, in addition to designing the cover of the catalog. I am indebted also to Ralph Jaeckel and Lee Blackburn for lending photographs for the exhibition and to Michel Ecochard who kindly allowed me to have prints made from some of his original glass negatives of Bonfils photographs, three of which are exhibited, and Studio Dorka of Paris which gave me a print of a Bonfils photograph which is included in the exhibition.

Los Angeles
October, 1981

Paul E. Chevedden

13. Portrait of Francis Frith in Turkish summer costume (Frith, 1857)

THE PHOTOGRAPHIC HERITAGE
OF THE MIDDLE EAST

Early Photographers in the Middle East

The history of photography and the Middle East are intimately intertwined. Just months after the first successful photographic process was developed in 1839, known as the daguerreotype after its inventor, Louis-Mandé Daguerre (1787-1851), N. P. Lerebours, a Paris optician and publisher, dispatched a group of daguerreotypists to Egypt and Palestine to bring back views of these lands which so evoked the romantic and religious interests of nineteenth century Europe. Among these early daguerreotypists were Frédéric Goupil-Fesquet and the painter Horace Vernet whose views appeared in Lerebour's *Excursions Daguerriennes, vues et monuments les plus remarquables du globe* (1841-44), the first publication with illustrations originally captured by the camera. The daguerreotype process used a silver-coated copper plate, sensitized with a thin coat of silver iodide, and produced direct positive pictures after a minimum exposure of several minutes. Since these images were unique and could not be reproduced, printed copies of them could only be made by artists converting them into etchings or lithographs. As a consequence, the photographic magic of a mirrored image was lost when the daguerreotypes were transformed for publication.

A new photographic process, the calotype, was invented in England by William Henry Fox Talbot at about the same time Daguerre published his process, but it was not perfected until about 1845 through the further work of Talbot and two Frenchmen working independently, Gustave Le Gray and L.-D. Blanquart-Evrard. These two photographic processes, the daguerreotype and calotype, were in competition throughout the 1840s until the calotype superseded and replaced the daguerreotype process by the latter part of the decade. The calotype process as it was developed and refined had distinct advantages over the daguerreotype, since it produced an image on light-sensitized paper which could be contact printed onto another sheet of sensitized paper. This created a positive image which was capable of being reproduced many times over. By the early 1850s hundreds of prints could be reproduced from a single negative, allowing for the first time the mass production and publication of original photographs.

The first photographer to utilize this process in the Middle East was Maxime Du Camp, who was sent on an official mission by the French Ministry of Education in 1849, accompanied by his friend, Gustave Flaubert, to photograph sites in Egypt and the Holy Land. The result of his labors, *Egypte, Nubie, Palestine et Syrie*, published by Gide and Baudry with 125 prints processed by Blanquart-Evrard, was a stunning success and is considered a landmark in the history of illustrated books, being one of the first truly ambitious publications illustrated fully with original photographs. Other calotypists soon followed Du Camp, among them being: Félix Teynard, who made two trips to Egypt in 1851-52 and 1869 and published 160 of his photographs in his work, *Egypte et Nubie, sites et monuments les plus intéressant pour l'étude de l'art et de l'histoire* (1853-58); John Bulkley Greene, who traveled to Egypt in the early 1850s and produced a two-volume publication, *Le Nil, monuments, paysages, exploitations photographiques* (1854); Auguste Salzmann, who journeyed to Jerusalem in 1853 and made a photographic study of the city published in 1856 under the title, *Jerusalem. Etude et reproduction photographique de monuments de la Ville Sainte*; and Louis de Clercq who accompanied the French archaeological expedition to the Middle East in 1859 headed by the famous historian of Crusader architecture, Emmanuel Guillaume Rey, and published a series of albums under the general title of *Voyage en Orient . . . 1859-1860* in five volumes, containing 177 photographs of Syria, Palestine, and Egypt.

A new photographic process developed by Frederick Scott Archer in 1851 superseded both the daguerreotype and calotype processes, and since it was not patented, gave a great impetus to the expansion of photography. Known as the wet collodion process, it used glass negative plates which the photographer coated with silver salts in collodion, and after exposing the glass plate while the coating was still wet, the latent image was immediately developed before the emulsion had time to dry. The clarity and detail of prints made from collodion glass negatives were far superior to those achieved by the daguerreotype or calotype processes. In addition, the wet collodion glass negatives were more permanent than the paper calotype negatives and photographs could be dependably mass produced from them on albumen-coated paper in far greater quantity. This new photographic process transformed the production of photographs and photographic publications into a large scale business enterprise. Because the wet collodion process required topographical photographers to travel with a portable darkroom, efforts were made to produce a dry collodion plate. J. M. Taupenot, a French chemist, developed a process by which this was achieved in 1855 in which the collodion was coated with a layer of iodized albumen, and in 1856 Dr. Hill Norris of Birmingham patented his own dry collodion process. Although the dry collodion process achieved considerable popularity, the wet collodion process remained in much wider use, owing to the fact that it was unpatented and required less exposure than the collodion dry-plates. The wet collodion process was finally superseded during the 1880s by the gelatin dry plate process from which all later photographic processes are derived.

The first noted photographer to use the wet collodion process was Francis Frith, the most well known of the more than one hundred photographers who worked in the Middle East during the nineteenth century. Frith made three trips to the Middle East—in 1856-57 to Egypt, in 1857-58 to Palestine and Syria, and in 1859-60 to Egypt, the Sinai, Transjordan, Palestine, Syria, Turkey (Smyrna and Istanbul), and Greece. The photographs which he brought back were published in a number of lavish volumes which were highly acclaimed and immensely popular. At roughly the same time as Frith came the German, W. Hammerschmidt, who photographed in Egypt and the Holy Land, and two Englishmen, James Robertson and his brother-in-law, Felice Beato, who made a photographic tour through Syria, Palestine, and Egypt on their way to photograph the Indian Revolt of 1857-58. In 1862 the photographer Francis Bedford was invited by Queen Victoria to accompany the Prince of Wales (later King Edward VII) on his tour of Egypt and the Holy Land and published 172 of the pictures taken on this trip in a deluxe four volume publication, *Photographic Pictures Made by Francis Bedford during the Tour of the East, in which by Command He Accompanied H.R.H. the Prince of Wales*.

Local Studios and Resident Photographers

Not long after the first wave of traveling photographers came to the Middle East, resident photographers established themselves there in many of the major cities and opened studios to cater to the ever growing demand for photographs of the Middle East. In Jerusalem the Englishmen, James Graham and Peter E. Bergheim, the Italian, Ermette Pierotti, and the Armenian Patriarch, Yessayi Garabedian, were active during the latter part of the 1850s, soon to be followed in the 1860s by Shapira and C. Krikorian. Toward the end of the century Nicodemus, Hentschel, and the American Colony had established studios. The photographic department of the American Colony was started by Frederich Vester and Elijah Meyers in 1898 to meet the demand for photographic mementos of the Imperial visit of Kaiser Wilhelm II of Germany. For the next half century it remained in operation, from 1934 onward under the able direction of Eric and Edith Matson. The 20,000 negatives produced over this period, now in the Library of Congress, constitute an invaluable pictorial record of the people, places, and events in the Middle East for the first half of this century.

In Beirut, Tancrède R. Dumas was the first to establish a studio in the early 1860s, followed in 1867 by Félix Bonfils and his wife, Lydie. The studio, La Maison Bonfils, established by Félix and Lydie and later managed by their son, Adrien, produced tens of thousands of photographs and several deluxe albums forming one of the most extensive visual records of the Middle East.

In Egypt, numerous studios were established throughout the second half of the nineteenth century. Antonio Beato came to Luxor in 1862 and established a studio which was well known for its prodigious output and excellent quality. In Cairo, studios proliferated and those of O. Schoefft, Stronmeyer, G. Lekegian, Heymann & Co., and Laroche & Co. are but a few that were established. In Port Saʿīd, H. Arnoux and G. Zangaki set up studios to capitalize on the brisk tourist traffic through the Suez Canal.

In Istanbul, the oldest known photographs taken of the city are those by E. Caranza dating from 1852. An Armenian photographic firm, known as Abdullah Frères, was established in the early 1850s, and its members became the first official photographers to the Ottoman court. This firm was instrumental in instructing other photographers, like Yessayi Garabedian, who in turn trained a number of other Armenian photographers who worked in the Middle East. The English photographers, James Robertson, and his associate, Felice Beato, worked in Istanbul during the early 1850s, producing many excellent photographs of the city, in addition to views of Malta and Greece, and became the first war photographers after the Rumanian, Carol Popp (de) Szàthmari, and the Englishman, Roger Fenton, in the Crimean War of 1854-56. Various other photographers such as Kargopulo and G. Berggren, and the photographic firm of Phoebus were active in Istanbul

102. The Great Temple of Ramses II at Abu Simbel (A. Beato, after 1875)

3

which so preoccupied the mind and imagination of nineteenth century Europe, was an image fashioned in the vision of the West through the poetry of Victor Hugo, Gerald de Nerval, Heinrich Heine, and Lord Byron, and transfixed on canvas by Eugène Delacroix, Théodore Chassériau, Eugène Fromentin, Jean-Léon Gérôme, and many others. The picturesque, exotic, and unchanging image which was portrayed of the Middle East was an illusion, but it was this illusion which the vast majority of commercial photographers, as much as the poets and artists, sought to capture and market in the West to a public which reveled in the romantic look of the Orient. The western image of the Middle East defined the subject matter of their photography and was restricted almost exclusively to the fallen grandeur of its past civilizations, its biblical antiquities and associations, and the inhabitants of the area insofar as they were picturesque or illustrative of how things must have been 2,000 or more years before. The remarks of Adrien Bonfils typify the thoughts and aims of many of the photographers who worked in the Middle East during the nineteenth century: "Costumes! Types! Customs!," he exclaims, "Everything seems fixed in this immutable Orient as if to confirm for us, even in most minute details, the authenticity and sincerity of what the Evangelists have told us. . . . Twenty centuries have passed without changing the decor and physiognomy of this land unique among all; but let us hasten if we wish to enjoy the sight. Progress, the great Trifler, will have swiftly brought about the destruction of what time itself has respected. Civilization, penetrating everywhere, will finish by taking away from this country, as it has from others, its character and special 'cachet'. A day will come when this land like all the others will perish. . . . Before that happens, before progress has completely done its destructive job, before this present which is still the past has forever disappeared, we have tried, so to speak, to fix and immobilize it in a series of photographic views we are offering to our readers in this album."*

The early photographic heritage of the Middle East mirrors the West's perception of the region as seen for the first time through the camera's eye, and reflects as much the audience which perceived it as the subject perceived. It provides a remarkable view of the Middle East of the nineteenth century which has indeed disappeared forever, and illustrates the marvels of the camera which from its first inception was able not only to record reality but compose and refashion it according to the vision of its practitioners.

The Exhibition

The photographs on exhibit are from albums in the Department of Special Collections at the UCLA Research Library and a few loaned by private collectors for this exhibition. Current articles and books on early photography of the Middle East are also exhibited. Although the number of early photographs of the Middle East in the Department of Special Collections is relatively modest (comprising 1,224 photographic prints), some of the most important photographers are represented with a considerable quantity of their work: Du Camp, Frith, Hammerschmidt, Bedford, A. Beato, and Zangaki.

Note: Captions for the photographs are taken directly from the descriptions accompanying the photographs, either written on the mount, on the print, or in the accompanying text, so deviations from standard orthography do occur. If a translation, correction, or further explanation is required, this is supplied in brackets. The first number listed under the caption is the page number of the mount or the number by which the photograph is identified in the negative file of the Department of Special Collections. The second number, appearing in parenthesis, is the number found on the print, inscribed by the photographer on the negative. The dimensions of the print are given in meters. If the print is inscribed with the name of the photographer or photographic firm, this name is given as it appears on the print, followed by the date if this is recorded on the print or mount. All prints and albums belong to the UCLA Department of Special Collections unless otherwise noted.

*Quoted in "The Photographers Bonfils of Beirut and Alès, 1867-1916" by C.E.S. Gavin, E. Carella, and I. O'Reilly in *Camera* 60 (March 1891):14.

MAXIME DU CAMP

In 1849 Maxime Du Camp (1822-1894) was commissioned by the French Ministry of Education to conduct an excursion through Egypt and the Holy Land in order to obtain photographs of the monuments and squeezes of historical inscriptions in these lands. His friend, Gustave Flaubert (1821-1880), who accompanied him on this expedition, was commissioned by the Ministry of Agriculture and Commerce to assess the economic potential of the regions visited. Du Camp dutifully carried out his assignment, taking over 200 photographs in Egypt, Nubia, Palestine, and Syria between November 1849 and September 1850, while Flaubert paid "no more attention to [his] mission than to the King of Prussia." Flaubert found other pursuits more enticing and so spent his days living "like a plant, filling [himself] with sun and light colors and fresh air. . . . " His correspondence and travel notes written during the course of the trip, however, provide a detailed and entertaining record of the expedition, far more illuminating than Du Camp's own writings, and these have been nicely compiled and translated by Francis Steegmuller (*Flaubert in Egypt: A Sensibility on Tour*. Boston and Toronto: Little, Brown & Co., 1972).

Following Du Camp's return to France he started making prints from his paper negatives, but was unable to retard the process of fading which eventually set in and deadened the lively effect of his photographs. During the middle of 1851, probably acting on the advice of his publishers, Gide and Baudry, Du Camp handed the printing of his photographs over to Blanquart-Evrard, who had just devised a new process for making permanent prints resistant to fading, utilizing albumen from chicken eggs to adhere the light-sensitive silver salts to the paper print and applying gold salts as a toning agent. The success of Blanquart-Evrard's new process is attested to by the fact that even today the 125 prints of Du Camp published in *Egypte, Nubie, Palestine et Syrie. Dessins photographiques recueillis pendant les années 1849, 1850 et 1851, accompagnés d'un texte explicatif et précédes d'une introduction par Maxime Du Camp* (Paris: Gide et J. Baudry, 1852) remain virtually unfaded.

The three-volume edition of Du Camp's photographs in the Department of Special Collections, containing 175 photographic prints, was produced privately by Du Camp before he consigned the printing of his negatives to Blanquart-Evrard. Fading, unfortunately, has claimed most of the prints, but nonetheless, this early edition of Du Camp's photographs contains the largest number of photographs taken on his expedition to the Middle East.* The title page of volume 1 carries a presentation note written by Du Camp: "Au grand artiste Bida," signed, "l'humble Photographe, Maxime Du Camp," Bernard Marbot, the curator of early photography in the Département des Estampes et de la Photographie de la Bibliothèque Nationale, has identified the person to whom Du Camp presented this album as Alexandre Bida (1823-95), a pupil of Eugène Delacroix who achieved success as an Orientalist painter, noted particularly for his drawings, and, like Du Camp, was part of the artistic and literary milieu of the period. The captions for all of the photographs in these three volumes are written in Du Camp's own hand.

*There are two other known pre-publication copies of Du Camp's photographs of the Middle East: Du Camp's own personal copy in the Bibliothèque de l'Institut de France and a copy in the Gilman Paper Company Collection, once owned by Viollet-le-Duc.

Du Camp's presentation note and signature on the title page of *Egypte, Nubie, Syrie: paysages & monuments:* "Au grand artiste Bida/l'humble Photographe/Maxime Du Camp."

DU CAMP, MAXIME
Egypte, Nubie, Syrie: paysages & monuments
3 volumes, n.p., 1851

Volume 1:
  58 mounted salt prints from calotype negatives
  Volume: 0.30 x 0.39 m
  Image: ca. 0.16 x 0.21 m

  1. *Le Caire: Maisons arabes*
      [Cairo, Flaubert in the courtyard of the Hòtel
      du Nil]
      5   0.148 x 0.205

  2. *Le Caire: Mosquee de Sultan Hasan*
      [Cairo, the Mosque of Sulṭān Ḥasan (1356-62)]
      7   0.16 x 0.212

  3. *Le Sphyns (abou-el-hoûl) vu de face*
      [The Sphinx, known in Arabic as Abū Hawl
      (the Father of Terror)]
      22   0.159 x 0.214

  4. *Denderah: sculptures de la façade posterieure
      du temple d'Athor*
      [Dendera, sculptures on the posterior facade of
      the Temple of Hathor]
      46   0.162 x 0.222

Volume 2:
  59 mounted salt prints from calotype negatives
  Volume: 0.30 x 0.393 m
  Image: ca. 0.16 x 0.21 m

  5. *Karnac. Pilier du Sanctuaire de granit, Tothmès
      III et la déesse Athor*
      [Karnak, Pillar in the Festival Temple of Thut-
      mose III, showing Thutmose III and the god-
      dess Hathor]
      65   0.164 x 0.209

  6. *Gournah. Portique du Ramesseum, Tombeau
      d'Asymandias*
      [Thebes, Mortuary Temple of Ramses II (the
      Ramasseum) and the fallen statue of Ramses
      II]
      75   0.17 x 0.224

  7. *Gournah. Statue Monolithe d'Amenophis III*
      [Thebes, Colossus of Memnon, one of two
      statues remaining from the Mortuary Temple of
      Amenhotep III]
      79   0.163 x 0.198

  8. *Medinet-habou. Propylées du Thoutmoseum*
      [Madīnat Habū, Entrance to the Small Temple,
      originally built by Amenhotep I and added on
      to by Hatshepsut and Thutmose III]
      82   0.165 x 0.214

Volume 3:
  58 mounted salt prints from calotype negatives
  Volume: 0.295 x 0.39 m
  Image: ca. 0.16 x 0.21 m

  9. *Kalabcheh: ensemble des Ruines du Temple*
      [The Temple of Kalābsha, built during the reign
      of Emperor Augustus (30-14 B.C.)]
      128   0.166 x 0.22

  10. *Kalabcheh. Sculptures de la façade posterieure
       —Portrait de Ptolémée Caesarion*
       [The Temple of Kalābsha. Relief of the Emper-
       or Augustus burning incense before Isis, Horus
       (pictured in no. 11), and Mandulis, on the rear
       wall of the sanctuary]
       130   0.166 x 0.224

  11. *Kalabcheh. Sculptures de la façade posterieure
       du Temple—Isis et Horus*
       [The Temple of Kalābsha. Relief of Isis and
       Horus on the rear wall of the sanctuary]
       131   0.168 x 0.228

  12. *Absamboul. Entrée du speos de Phré*
       [The entrance to the Great Temple of Ramses
       II at Abu Simbel]
       151   0.168 x 0.218

12. The entrance to the Great Temple of Ramses II
     at Abu Simbel (Du Camp, 1850)

Francis Frith (1822-1898) started out at 23 in the grocery wholesale business in Liverpool, worked hard, saved his money, and opened a printing house which he sold in 1856 for a substantial profit. At 34, as a man of independent means, he settled into the life of a country gentleman. But leisure did not suit Francis Frith. Sometime in the early 1850s Frith had taken up "the Black Art," as photography was deridingly called in those days, and with an itch to break with his aimless ways set off loaded with photographic gear on a "quest towards the romantic and perfected past." He arrived in Egypt in September 1856 and sailed up the Nile as far as Abu Simbel and then retraced his journey photographing in earnest as he went. When his photographs were exhibited in England upon his return in July 1857, they received rave reviews and publication of them soon began in fascicle form under the title, *Egypt and Palestine Photographed and Described by Francis Frith* (London: J. S. Virtue, 1858-60, 2 vols., issued in 25 parts, containing 76 albumen prints). In November 1857 Frith was off again to the Middle East, this time to Palestine and Syria, where he photographed busily until May of the following year. The photographs from these two trips appear in *Egypt and Palestine Photographed and Described*, which was completed in the spring of 1860 in an edition of 2,000.

The Department of Special Collections has three copies of *Egypt and Palestine Photographed and Described*. The first copy contains 76 albumen prints with no descriptive text accompanying the photographs. The second and third copies contain 76 and 75 albumen prints respectively, interleaved with a descriptive text

54. Petra, the arch over the Great Ravine (Frith, 1860)

19 & 20. Panorama of Jerusalem from the Mount of Olives (Frith, 1857)

of one or two pages for each photograph. The selection of sites photographed in these three copies is for the most part the same, but the views selected of these sites in some cases differ and the arrangement of the photographs varies slightly in all three copies. Sixty-two photographs, made from the same negative, are found in all three copies, 12 photographs are reproduced in two of the copies, and 16 photographs appear only in one of the copies, making a total of 90 different prints in all. Nearly all of the 16 unique prints are variant views of the same sites pictured in one or two of the other copies. One curious exception is a photograph of the East Gate of Damascus in copy 3 (no. 23). The accompanying descriptive text to this photograph states that it is a general view of Damascus (not the East Gate) taken

from a roof near the East Gate. The photograph with the same descriptive text in copies 1 and 2 (copies 1 & 2, no. 22) is a rooftop view of Damascus, but it is taken from Sufl at-Talla nearly 600 meters away from the East Gate. Four of the prints in copy 2 are affixed to the wrong mount so the captions do not match the photographs (copy 2, nos. 36, 39, 40 and 56). The mounts in all three copies carry captions and are identified and dated, "Frith Photo 1857." Most of the prints are also signed, numbered, and dated by Frith.

In the late summer of 1859 Frith embarked on what was to be his most ambitious and extensive tour through the Middle East which lasted well into the following year. He traveled up the Nile beyond the second cataract to the Temple of Ṣūlb, further than any photographer

had been before, crossed the Sinai via the southern route, passed through Petra to Palestine and Syria, and arrived finally in Jaffa where he boarded a steamer and continued on to Smyrna, Istanbul, and Greece.

Upon his return to England in 1860, Frith produced nine more books of photographs using pictures taken on all three trips. A four-volume collection of his photographs, containing 148 albumen prints, was published by William Mackenzie in 1862, each volume designated by region: *Sinai and Palestine*; *Lower Egypt, Thebes, and the Pyramids*; *Upper Egypt and Ethiopia*; and *Egypt, Sinai, and Palestine, Supplementary Volume*. Two of these volumes, *Sinai and Palestine* and *Lower Egypt, Thebes, and the Pyramids*, are in the Department of Special Collections. The largest single collection of

photographs of Frith's third and final trip to the Middle East is also in the Department of Special Collections. These photographs, 114 in number, are on letterpress mounts with captions and in many cases Biblical citations tying the pictures directly to a Biblical context. Such Biblical citations are also printed on all of the mounts of the 56 Frith photographs published in *The Queen's Bible* (Glasgow: W. MacKenzie, 1862-63). Although none of the 114 photographs carries any identification of authorship, they are all clearly the product of Frith's third tour of the Middle East. They concur exactly with his itinerary and include views of many of the sites he previously photographed on earlier trips. A number of these photographs are almost mirror images of the earlier ones, i.e., The Pool of Hezekiah

13

(no. 572), Nablous (no. 590), Banias (no. 603), Baalbek, Circular Temple (no. 611), Baalbek, the Great Pillars (no. 613), Cairo, from the East (no. 649), and Tombs in the Southern Cemetery, Cairo (no. 650). In addition, some of the captions to these photographs are identical with those on earlier photographs and the spelling of place names is the same.

To produce the large numbers of prints to illustrate his many publications, Frith established a printing firm at Reigate, known as F. Frith & Co., which became one of the largest photographic publishers in the world. Frith went on to become one of the leading commercial landscape photographers in Britain, photographing countless cities, towns, and villages in England, Scotland, Wales, and Ireland. After his death in 1898, Frith & Co. continued production of photographic prints and postcards under the management of Frith's children and their descendants until 1968 when the firm was sold. Three years later the new management declared bankruptcy and Frith & Co. was no more.

FRITH, FRANCIS
Egypt and Palestine Photographed and Described
2 vols in 1, London: J. S. Virtue, n.d. [1858-60], copy 1

76 mounted albumen prints
Volume: 0.315 x 0.435 m
Image: ca. 0.16 x 0.23 m

13. *Portrait* [of Francis Frith in] *Turkish Summer costume*
    1   0.144 x 0.182   1857

14. *The Pool of Hezekiah, etc. from the Tower of Hippicus*
    [The Pool of the Patriarch's Bath (Birkat Hammām al-Baṭrak) and the Church of the Holy Sepulchre from the Tower of Phasael, known from the Byzantine period onward as the Tower of David]
    4 (P 117)   0.165 x 0.233   Frith 1857

15. *Cleopatra's Temple at Erment*
    5 (E 41)   0.163 x 0.228   Frith 1857

16. *Sculptures from the Outer Wall, Dendera*
    10 (E 13)   0.161 x 0.228   Frith 1857

17. *Abou Simbel, Nubia*
    [The Great Temple of Ramses II at Abu Simbel]
    15 (E 7)   0.151 x 0.219   Frith 1857

18. *Osidride Pillars and Great Fallen Colossus, The Memnonium, Thebes*
    [Thebes, the Ramasseum and the fallen statue of Ramses II]
    17 (E 58)   0.161 x 0.225   Frith 1857

19. *Jerusalem, from the Mount of Olives, no. 1*
    52 (P 101)   0.157 x 0.229   Frith 1857

20. *Jerusalem, from the Mount of Olives, no. 2*
    52 (P 102)   0.156 x 0.23   Frith 1857

21. *Assouan*
    [Aswān]
    59 (E 35)   0.159 x 0.228   Frith 1857

FRITH, FRANCIS
Egypt and Palestine Photographed and Described
2 vols. in 1, London: J. S. Virtue, n.d. [1858-60], copy 2

76 mounted albumen prints interleaved with descriptive text of one or two pages for each photograph
Volume: 0.31 x 0.433 m
Image: ca. 0.16 x 0.23 m

22. *The Temple of Wady Kardassy, Nubia*
    [The Temple of Kartassi, re-erected at Shallāl, a few miles from Aswān]
    42 (E 19)   0.165 x 0.23   Frith 1857

FRITH, FRANCIS
Egypt and Palestine Photographed and Described
2 vols. in 1, London: J. S. Virtue, n.d. [1858-60], copy 3, (Title page, contents, and a list of subscribers missing)

75 mounted albumen prints interleaved with descriptive text of one or two pages for each photograph
Volume: 0.31 x 0.428 m
Image: ca. 0.16 x 0.23 m

23. *Damascus*
    [Damascus, East Gate (Bāb Sharqī)]
    20 (P 128)   0.159 x 0.225   Frith 1857

FRITH, FRANCIS
Sinai and Palestine
Awarded a Prize Medal. London: W. MacKenzie, n.d. [1862]

37 mounted albumen prints interleaved with descriptive text of one or two pages for each photograph
Volume: 0.315 x 0.437 m
Image: ca. 0.16 x 0.225 m

24. *The Street Called Straight, Damascus*
    [The Roman *decumanus*, first mentioned in Acts 9:11. View taken through the northern bay of the East Gate (Bab Sharqi)]
    1   0.117 x 0.146

25. *The Convent of Sinai and Plain of er-Raha*
    [The Monastery of St. Catherine in the Sinai]
    4 (182)   0.157 x 0.225   Frith

26. *Hebron with Mosque covering the Cave of Macpelah*
    9 (P 119)   0.159 x 0.225   Frith

27. *Gaza (The Old Town)*
    10 (190)   0.159 x 0.226   Frith

28. *The Mosque of Aksa, Jerusalem*
[Jerusalem, The al-Aqṣā Mosque on the Temple Mount taken from the southern walls of the city]
14   0.159 x 0.228   Frith

29. *Street view with the Church of the Holy Sepulchre, Jerusalem*
19 (190)   0.158 x 0.227   Frith

30. *Mosque of Omar etc., Jerusalem*
[Jerusalem, The Dome of the Rock, the first major Islamic monument, built by ʿAbd al-Malik between 688 and 691]
22 (P 108)   0.158 x 0.224   Frith

31. *Nablous. The Ancient Shechem*
27 (P 134)   0.163 x 0.225   Frith

32. *The Great Pillars and Smaller Temple, Baalbec*
[Baalbek, the columns of the Temple of Jupiter Heliopolitan (foreground) and the Temple of Bacchus in the distance]
35 (P 143)   0.164 x 0.228   Frith

FRITH, FRANCIS
Lower Egypt, Thebes, and the Pyramids
Awarded a Prize Medal. London: W. MacKenzie, n.d. [1862]

38 mounted albumen prints interleaved with descriptive text of one or two pages for each photograph
Volume: 0.315 x 0.437 m
Image: ca. 0.16 x 0.225 m

33. *Travellers Boat at Ibrim*
1   0.137 x 0.17   Frith

34. *Cairo, from the East*
[Cairo, city wall and tower constructed by Saladin on the eastern side of the city. Monu-

56. The Monastery of Mār Sābā located midway between Jerusalem and the Dead Sea (Frith, 1860)

ments in the foreground left to right are: Palace of Ālīn Āq (1293), Mosque of Khayrbak (1502), and Mosque of Ibrāhīm Āghā Mustaḥfiẓān (1346-47). Monuments in background are: the Mosque of Sulṭān Ḥasan (1356-62) on the left and the Mosque of Ylgāy al-Yūsufī (1373) on the right]
2 (90)   0.162 x 0.224

35. *Tombs in the Southern Cemetery, Cairo*
[Cairo, Cemetery of the Mamluks, south of the Citadel. Monuments from left to right are: Mosque of Nūr ad-Dīn (1575), Mausoleum of ʿAlī Badr ad-Dīn al-Qarāfī and the Southern Minaret (ca. 1300-10), Mosque of Muḥammad ʿAlī (1848), Minaret of the Khāngāh of Amīr Qawṣūn (1336), Northern Minaret of as-Sulṭān-īya Mausoleum (14th century), unidentified mausoleum, destroyed ca. 1859 (late 14th century), unidentified mausoleum, as-Sulṭānīya Mausoleum (14th century), Khāngāh and Mausoleum of Amīr Qawṣūn (1336), Mausoleum of Amir Sūdūn (1504-05), and Qubbat aṣ-Ṣawābī (ca 1285-86)]
4 (79)   0.16 x 0.228   Frith

36. *The Ezebeeyeh, Cairo*
[Cairo, Coptic houses along the northeast corner of the Azbakīya Gardens]
5   0.159 x 0.22   Frith

37. *The Citadel of Cairo*
[The Citadel of Cairo and the Mosque of Muḥammad ʿAlī from the Muqaṭṭam Hills to the southeast]
9   0.158 x 0.226   Frith

38. *Street View in Cairo*
[Cairo, Street view along the Darb al-Aḥmar with the minarets of the Mosques of Ibrāhīm Āghā Mustaḥfiẓān (1346-47) and Khayrbak (1502) in the background]
10   0.16 x 0.205   Frith

39. *The Great Pyramid and the Sphinx*
11   0.158 x 0.23   Frith

40. *The Pyramids of el-Geezeh* [Giza]
12   0.159 x 0.225   Frith

41. *The Pyramids of Sakkarah* [Saqqāra]
13   0.159 x 0.218   Frith 1856

42. *The Pyramids of Dashoor* [Dahshūr]
14 (156)   0.159 x 0.228   Frith

43. *Cleopatra's Temple at Erment*
17   0.158 x 0.228   Frith

44. *Valley of the Tombs of the Kings, Thebes*
29   0.16 x 0.226   Frith

45. *Pylon Gateway at Medinet-Habou, Thebes*
23   0.163 x 0.222   Frith

46. *Entrance to the Great Temple, Luxor*
28   0.156 x 0.222   Frith

47. *The Court of Shishak, Karnac*
[Karnak, Second Pylon, fronting the Great

Hypostyle Hall, built by Ramses II and restored by the Ptolemies]
36 (E 68)   0.16 x 0.22   Frith 1857

48. *Interior of the Hall of Columns, Karnac*
[Karnak, Interior of the Great Hypostyle Hall]
37   0.16 x 0.226   Frith

FRITH, FRANCIS
114 albumen prints on letterpress mounts of the Sinai (15), Transjordan (7), Palestine (38), Syria (9), Turkey [Smyrna] (1), Greece (22), and Egypt [Cairo and the Pyramids] (22), numbered 521-622 (missing numbers 522, 526, 530, 534, 543-45, 547, 549-51, 553-56, 558, 562, 579, 591, 596, 606-07, 610, 612, 614-16, 657). n.p., n.d. [Photographs date from 1859-60]
Mount: 0.294 x 0.353 m
Image: ca. 0.156 x 0.208 m

49. *The Written Valley, Sinai (Wady Mukatteb), containing the mysterious Sinaitic inscriptions in great numbers*
525   0.154 x 0.208

50. *The Convent of Mount Sinai*
[The Monastery of St. Catherine in the Sinai]
536   0.154 x 0.209

51. *Hazeroth (Hudera)*
537   0.154 x 0.209

52. *Defile, near the Red Sea (Wady el-Ain)*
[Defile in the Sinai, near the Gulf of Aqaba (Wādi Watīr)]
538   0.157 x 0.209

53. *Craia, on the Red Sea, near Eziongeber*
[Jazīrat Firʿawn (Pharoah's Island) in the Gulf of Aqaba, some 14 km. southwest of the town of Aqaba. The fortress on its summit was constructed by Baldwin I in 1116]
539   0.147 x 0.203

54. *Arch over the Great Ravine, Petra*
546   0.158 x 0.209

55. *Bethlehem, from the Latin Convent*
560   0.153 x 0.206

56. *The Wilderness of Engedi, the Convent of Mar Saba*
564   0.157 x 0.209

57. *Jerusalem, from the Mount of Olives, looking over the Valley of Jehoshaphat*
566   0.156 x 0.209

58. *Pool of Hezekiah, and Church of the Holy Sepulchre, Jerusalem*
[The Pool of the Patriarch's Bath (Birkat Hammām al-Baṭrak) and the Church of the Holy Sepulchre]
572   0.149 x 0.207

59. *Façade of the Church of the Holy Sepulchre, Jerusalem*
580   0.157 x 0.206

60. *Mosque of Omar, Jerusalem, from the West, on the site of Solomon's Temple*

[Jerusalem, The Dome of the Rock built by the Caliph ʿAbd al-Malik between 688 and 691]
582   0.158 x 0.21

61. *Mosque of Aksa, Jerusalem*
[Jerusalem, the entrance facade of the al-Aqṣā Mosque]
586   0.157 x 0.206

62. *Nazareth, from the West, with the distant summit of Mount Tabor*
594   0.157 x 0.207

63. *Tiberias and the Sea of Galilee*
600   0.143 x 0.206

64. *Damascus, with the Great Mosque*
608   0.153 x 0.206

65. *Athens, with the Acropolis*
619   0.157 x 0.207

66. *The Parthenon, Athens, from the West*
625   0.154 x 0.207

67. *The Obelisk of On (Heliopolis)*
640   0.157 x 0.202

68. *Shipping on the Banks of the Nile*
641   0.159 x 0.203

69. *The Great Pyramid and Sphinx*
643   0.154 x 0.205

70. *The Great Pyramid and Excavated Temple*
644   0.154 x 0.207

71. *Pyramid of Dashour* [Dahshūr]
645   0.151 x 0.25

72. *Valley of the Nile, and the Pyramids*
647   0.152 x 0.207

73. *Cairo, from the Citadel with the Mosque of Sultan Hassan*
648   0.154 x 0.207

74. *Cairo, from the East*
[Cairo, city wall and tower constructed by Saladin on the eastern side of the city. Monuments

65.   View of Athens and the Acropolis (Frith, 1860)

17

68. Shipping on the banks of the Nile (Frith, 1859)

from left to right are: Palace of Ālīn Āq (1293), Mosque of Khayrbak (1502), and Mosque of Ibrāhīm Āghā Mustaḥfiẓān (1346-47)]
649   0.157 x 0.208

75. *Tombs of the Mamelukes, Cairo*
[Cairo, cemetery of the Mamluks, south of the Citadel. Monuments from left to right are: Mosque of Sulṭān Ḥasan (1356-62), Mosque of Nūr ad-Dīn (1575), Mausoleum of ʿAlī Badr ad-Din al-Qarāfī and the Southern Minaret (ca. 1300-10), Mosque of Muḥammad ʿAlī (1848), Minaret of the Khānqāh of Amīr Qawṣūn (1336), Northern Minaret of as-Sulṭānīya Mausoleum (14th century), unidentified mausoleum, as-Sulṭānīya Mausoleum (14th century), Khānqāh and Mausoleum of Amīr Qawṣūn (1336), Mausoleum of Amīr Sūdūn (1504-05), and Qubbat aṣ-Ṣawābī (ca. 1285-86)]
650   0.15 x 0.199

76. *Tombs of the Caliphs, Cairo*
[Cairo, Eastern Cemetery. Mausoleum of Khadīja Umm al-Ashraf (ca. 1430-40) in the foreground, and to the right of it in the distance, the Khānqāh of Faraj ibn Barqūq (1400-11) and the Khānqāh and Mosque of al-Ashraf Barsbay (1432)]
651   0.157 x 0.199

77. *Modern Tombs, Cairo*
[Cairo, the Cemetery of Bāb al-Wazīr on the northern side of the Citadel]
652   0.153 x 0.205

78. *Fountain in the Mosque of Sultan Hassan, Cairo*
654   0.158 x 0.206

79. *Street View, Cairo, from the Mosque of Sultan Hassan*
662   0.159 x 0.207

18

W. HAMMERSCHMIDT

Little is known of the German photographer, W. Hammerschmidt. He traveled to the Middle East prior to 1860 and photographed in both Egypt and Palestine. In Egypt, while attempting to photograph Muslim pilgrims on their way to Mecca in the desert outside of Cairo, Hammerschmidt was shot and severely wounded after having been warned not to take photographs. Bernard Marbot has found references to Hammerschmidt in the *Bulletin de la Société Française de Photographie* (1860) and in *La Lumière* (1860 and 1861) which indicate that he presented some of his photographs of Egypt to the Société Française de Photographie and used the dry collodion process developed by Taupenot.

The Department of Special Collections has two albums of his photographs of Egypt which include pictures of Alexandria, Cairo, the Pyramids, and sites in Upper Egypt as far as Abu Simbel: *Monuments de l'Egypte ancienne et moderne* (n.p., n.d.) and *Souvenirs d'Egypte* (Ernest Godard, 1862). All of the 54 albumen prints in *Souvenirs* are numbered and signed, "W. Hammerschmidt." Of the 83 albumen prints in *Monuments*, 80 are signed, "W. Hammerschmidt," but only 23 are numbered. The two albums share 52 prints in common, made from the same negative, but the numbering of these prints differs and in some cases two numbers are visible on the prints in *Souvenirs*—the same

88. The Sphinx (Hammerschmidt, 1858-59)

35. Cairo, Cemetery of the Mamluks, south of the Citadel (Frith, 1857)

80. Cairo, Cemetery of the Mamluks, south of the Citadel (Hammerschmidt, 1858-59)

75. Cairo, Cemetery of the Mamluks, south of the Citadel (Frith, 1859)

number as found on the identical print in *Monuments* and a new number. Hence, the original numbers, found on some of the prints in *Monuments*, were changed to a new and complete numbering system found on the prints in *Souvenirs*. This confirms that *Monuments*, for which no publisher or date is given, was issued prior to the publication of *Souvenirs* in 1862.

The highest number recorded on a print in these two albums is 90, on the photograph of the Great Temple of Abu Simbel in *Souvenirs* (*Souvenirs* no. 51), which indicates that Hammerschmidt took approximately 100 photographs in Egypt. Since there are no photographs in these albums of sites beyond Abu Simbel, it is most probable that this was the furthest point reached by Hammerschmidt on his trip up the Nile.

It is possible to date the photographs in these two albums as either 1857-58 or 1858-59, since some can be positively identified as being taken in the interval between Frith's first excursion to Egypt in 1856-57 and his last trip in 1859-60. Frith's photograph of the Cemetery of the Mamluks south of the Citadel of Cairo taken in 1857 (no. 35) shows a late fourteenth century mausoleum in the center of the picture with a ribbed dome composed of vertical bands in moulded relief which interlock at the base in a chain-like fashion. Hammerschmidt's photograph of this same area (no. 80)

shows the dome of this mausoleum completely destroyed with only part of the transition zone between the square tomb chamber and the circular drum of the dome remaining. In Frith's photograph of this area taken in 1859 (no. 75) all trace of the transition zone has vanished. Both Frith and Hammerschmidt took photographs of the Coptic houses along the northeast corner of the Azbakīya Gardens. Hammerschmidt's photograph of this area (no. 83) shows a new hotel on the extreme left which is absent from Frith's photograph taken in 1857 (no. 36). Both photographers took identical photographs of a Cairo street from the Mosque of Sulṭān Ḥasan, and the internal evidence indicates that Hammerschmidt's photograph (no. 82) predates Frith's photograph taken in 1859 (no. 79). Likewise, the panorama of Cairo taken by Hammerschmidt from the Citadel (nos. 97 & 98) predates the same view taken by Frith in 1859 (no. 73), and Hammerschmidt's photograph of the Cemetery of Bāb al-Wazīr and the northern side of the Citadel of Cairo (no. 93) was taken prior to a similar view taken by Frith in 1859 (no. 77).

In Upper Egypt both photographers took pictures of the *mammisi* or "birth temple" erected by Cleopatra at Erment. Hammerschmidt's photograph (no. 92) was taken after Frith's 1857 photograph (no. 15), but before his 1859 photograph (no. 43). Frith and

Hammerschmidt also took identical photographs of the Second Pylon fronting the Great Hypostyle Hall at the Temple of Karnak. The foreground of Frith's photograph taken in 1857 (no. 47) is filled with fallen debris, while Hammerschmidt's photograph was taken after the area had been cleared (no. 89).

These examples are sufficient to indicate that Hammerschmidt photographed in Egypt between Frith's first and last excursions to the country, dating his trip as the winter months of either 1857-58 or 1858-59; the latter date is probably the more likely.

HAMMERSCHMIDT, W.
Monuments de l'Egypte ancienne et moderne
n.p., n.d. [ca. 1860]
83 mounted albumen prints
Volume: 0.40 x 0.50 m
Image: ca. 0.235 x 0.312 m

80. *Le cimetière des Mamelouks*
[Cairo, Cemetery of the Mamluks, south of the Citadel. Monuments left to right are: Mausoleum of ʿAlī Badr ad-Dīn al-Qarāfī and the Southern Minaret (ca. 1300-10), Mosque of Muḥammad ʿAlī (1848), Minaret of Khānqāh of Amīr Qawṣūn (1336), Northern Minaret of as-Sulṭānīya Mausoleum (14th century), unidentified mausoleum with dome destroyed (late 14th century), unidentified mausoleum, and as-Sulṭānīya mausoleum (14th century)]
6 (6)   0.235 x 0.309   W. Hammerschmidt

81. *Mosquée du Sultan Asehraf*
[Cairo, Eastern Cemetery. Monuments left to right are: Khānqāh and Mosque of al-Ashraf Barsbāy (1432), Mausoleum of Jānī Bek al-Ashrafī (1427), Khānqāh and Mausoleum of Qurqumās (1506-07), and Mosque of Sulṭān Ināl (1451-56)]
13 (7)   0.235 x 0.314   W. Hammerschmidt

82. *Souk el-Sélah*
[Cairo, street view taken from the Mosque of Sulṭān Ḥasan]
18 (33)   0.236 x 0.31   W. Hammerschmidt

83. *Maison Coptes a l'Ezbékieh*
[Cairo, Coptic houses along the northeastern corner of the Azbakīya Gardens]
20 (9)   0.236 x 0.311   W. Hammerschmidt

84. *Le Kiosque de Schoubra*
[The Palace of Muḥammad ʿAlī in Shubrā, several miles north of the center of Cairo near the banks of the Nile, built between 1808 and 1809]
22 (25)   0.233 x 0.312   W. Hammerschmidt

85. *Vue générale des Pyramides de Ghyzéh*
[The Pyramids of Giza]
25   0.236 x 0.312   W. Hammerschmidt

86. *La grande Pyramide*
[The Pyramid of Cheops and the Sphinx (extreme right)]
26 (10)   0.237 x 0.31   W. Hammerschmidt

87. *La Pyramide de Céphren*
[The Pyramid of Chephren]
27 (11)   0.233 x 0.313   W. Hammerschmidt

88. *Le Sphinx*
[The Sphinx]
28 (12)   0.237 x 0.312   W. Hammerschmidt

89. *Première Cour du grand Temple de Karnak*
[Karnak, Second Pylon, fronting the Great Hypostyle Hall, built by Ramses II and restored by the Ptolemies]
38   0.237 x 0.309   W. Hammerschmidt

HAMMERSCHMIDT, W.
Souvenirs d'Egypte
Ernest Godard, 1862
54 mounted albumen prints
Volume: 0.362 x 0.446 m
Image: ca. 0.235 x 0.315 m

90. *Rhamessésum à Thébés, avec la statue de Sésosiris*
[Thebes, the Mortuary Temple of Ramses II (The Ramasseum), with the fallen statue of Ramses II on the left, which inspired Shelley's famous poem, "Ozymandias"]
2 (64)   0.238 x 0.312   W. Hammerschmidt

91. *Sultan Barkouk, Tombeau de Calife*
[Cairo, Eastern Cemetery, Khānqāh of Faraj ibn Barqūq (1400-11)]
3 (16)   0.235 x 0.313   W. Hammerschmidt

92. *Temple d'Hermonthis dans la Haute-Egypte*
[The *mammisi* or "birth temple" erected by Cleopatra at Erment]
7 (69)   0.24 x 0.315   W. Hammerschmidt

93. *Citadelle du Caire, Vue du Nord*
[Northern side of the Citadel of Cairo, taken from the Cemetery of Bāb al-Wazīr]
13 (13)   0.237 x 0.313   W. Hammerschmidt

94. *Colosses de Memnon à Thébés*
[Thebes, the Colossi of Memnon]
14 (63)   0.238 x 0.307   W. Hammerschmidt

95. *Boulaque, Faubourg du Caire*
[Būlāq, the main port of Cairo from the middle of the 15th century. It was separated from Cairo by fields and gardens and maintained an existence of its own until joined to the city during the middle of the 19th century]
17 (33)   0.224 x 0.317   W. Hammerschmidt

96. *Partie du Caire, vue du Minaret de la Mosquée Touloun*
[Cairo, view taken from the Minaret of the Mosque of Aḥmad ibn Ṭūlūn (876-79) looking southwest towards the Aqueduct and the Pyra-

mids of Giza beyond]
28 (9)   0.24 x 0.316   W. Hammerschmidt

97. *Vue générale du Caire, pris de la Citadelle. Partie gauche*
[View taken from the Citadel of Cairo, with the Mosque of Ṣultān Ḥasan (1356-62) in the foreground]
37 (8)   0.238 x 0.316   W. Hammerschmidt

98. *Vue générale du Caire, pris de la Citadelle. Partie droite*
[View taken from the Citadel of Cairo. Mosque of al-Maḥmūdīya (1568) on left, Mosque of Qānī-Bay Amīr Akhūr (1503) on right, and behind, the Mosque of Ylgāy al-Yūsufī (1373)]
41 (7)   0.238 x 0.315   W. Hammerschmidt

99. *Kaid Bey. Tombeau de Caliph*
[Cairo, Eastern Cemetery, Mosque and Mausoleum of Sulṭān Qaytbāy (1472-74)]
46 (20)   0.24 x 0.316   W. Hammerschmidt

100. *Rue de la Citadelle au Caire*
[The Darb al-Aḥmar leading from the Citadel to Bāb Zuwayla, with the Mosque of Aytmish al-Bagāsī (1383)]
48 (27)   0.24 x 0.317   W. Hammerschmidt

94.   Thebes, the Colossi of Memnon (Hammerschmidt, 1858-59)

Francis Bedford (1816-94) was a leading landscape and architectural photographer active in England during the 1850s and 1860s. In the early part of 1862, at the request of Queen Victoria, he accompanied the Prince of Wales (later King Edward VII) on his tour of Egypt, Palestine, Syria, Turkey, Greece, and the Mediterranean islands. He used 10" x 12" wet collodion negatives and took 210 photographs; 172 were printed in large format in four volumes by the lithographers to the Queen, Day & Son, as *Photographic Pictures made by Mr. Francis Bedford during the tour of the East, in which by command he accompanied H.R.H. the Prince of Wales* (1863). This publication was quite costly, so in 1864 Day & Son brought out a smaller and less expensive edition with reduced copies of 48 large photographs and a text by William M. Thompson. Thompson, an American missionary and traveler, was the author of *The Land and the Book*, the most popular American book of its time after *Uncle Tom's Cabin*; it was continually revised and reprinted throughout the second half of the nineteenth century.

101. The Departure of H. R. H. the Prince of Wales and Suite from the Pyramids (Bedford, 1862)

BEDFORD, FRANCIS
> *The Holy Land, Egypt, Constantinople, Athens, etc., etc. A Series of Forty-eight Photographs. Taken by Francis Bedford, for H.R.H. the Prince of Wales during the Tour of the East, in which, by Command, He Accompanied His Royal Highness*
> With descriptive text and introduction by W. M. Thompson, London: Day & Son, Ltd., n.d. [1864]
> X, 99 [1] pp.

48 mounted albumen prints
Volume: 0.189 x 0.243 m
Image: ca. 0.105 x 0.13 m

101. *The Departure of H.R.H. the Prince of Wales and Suite from the Pyramids*
p. 7, Pl. 1   0.105 x 0.125

Antonio Beato (d. 1903) arrived in Egypt in 1862 and established a photographic studio in Luxor. This studio, which operated well into the 1890s, was one of the most productive in the Middle East and produced a consistent quantity of excellent photographs, which were destined to fill tourists' albums. The Department of Special Collections possesses two such tourists' albums filled with Beato photographs compiled by the Vanderbilt party as a mememto of their excursion up the Nile during the winter of 1887-88. A large proportion of the 285 albumen prints in these two albums are signed, "A. Beato," and appear to date from the 1870s and early 1880s.

The first two photographs of the second album show the Vanderbilt party on board a Nile steamer. William Kissam Vanderbilt, his family, and a host of guests, including Winfield Scott Hoyt and Oliver Hazard Perry Belmont, are in attendance, but only Mrs. Alva Vanderbilt (later Mrs. O.H.P. Belmont), and her daughter, Consuelo, and son, Harold Stirling, are identified. William K. Vanderbilt was an ambitious sight-seer and largely ignored his wife for the splendors of ancient Egypt, leaving her in the company of Mr. Belmont, a bachelor of great wealth, charm, and good looks. In 1895 the Vanderbilts were divorced and Alva married Mr. Belmont in the following year. Alva went on to become one of the great leaders of the suffragette movement, head of the National Woman's party, and one of the most colorful women of her time. She died in Paris at the age of 80 on January 26, 1933.

BEATO, ANTONIO
[Two Tourists' Albums of Photographs of Egypt Taken by A. Beato, Compiled by the Vanderbilt Party upon Their Trip to Egypt during the Winter of 1887-88]

Volume 1:
98 mounted albumen prints on 98 pp.
Volume: 0.349 x 0.475 m
Image: ca. 0.265 x 0.38 m

102. *Nubie. Le grand Temple d'Ibsamboul*
[The Great Temple of Ramses II at Abu Simbel]
2   0.265 x 0.373   A. Beato

103. *Nubie. Le petit Temple d'Ibsamboul*
[The Small Temple at Abu Simbel, dedicated to Hathor and built by Ramses II as a tribute to his favorite wife, Nefertari]
3   0.264 x 0.383

Volume 2:
187 mounted albumen prints (7 missing) on 97 pp.
Volume: 0.352 x 0.478 m
Image: ca. 0.20 x 0.262 m

104. *Edfou. Le Sanctuaire*
[The Temple of Edfū, interior of the sanctuary. The monolithic shrine of polished grey granite, made by Nectanebos II of the XXXth Dynasty]
34 (L.)   0.20 x 0.262

105. *Edfou. Ptolomèe Philometor*
[The Temple of Edfū, outer corridor, east side. Nekhbet (right) and Wazit [Buto] (left) crowning Ptolemy Euregetes II]
34 (R.)   0.20 x 0.262

106. *Edfou. Bas reliefs interiéur du Temple*
[The Temple of Edfū, outer corridor, west side. Hathor and Atum conducting Ptolemy Euergetes II to Horus]
35 (L.)   0.201 x 0.263

107. *Edfou. La chasse de ramses*
[The Temple of Edfū, outer wall, west side, inner face. Horus in a boat catching the hind leg of a hippopotamus with a line while thrusting a harpoon into its snout. Isis squats in the bow holding the head of the animal with a rope. On land stands one of the Ptolemies plunging his harpoon into the neck of the animal]
35 (R.)   0.20 x 0.262

Félix Bonfils (1831-1885) first came to the Middle East with the French expeditionary force in 1860 which occupied the Lebanon for about a year following the civil strife between the Christians and Druzes in which thousands of Christians were massacred. Félix brought back such glowing reports of the Lebanon that his wife, Lydie (1837-1918), decided some years later to take their son, Adrien (1861-1929), there on the recommendation of a physician who suggested a sea voyage to a warm and dry climate to cure his chronic coughing. Lydie was so entranced by the beauty of the country that she persuaded her husband to move the family there permanently and set up a photographic studio as a means of support. The Bonfils family arrived in Beirut in 1867 and established *La Maison Bonfils* which in four years time produced 15,000 photographic prints made from 591 negatives of Egypt, Palestine, Syria, and Greece, in addition to 9,000 stereoscopic views. The prodigious output of the studio over its decades of operation was phenomenal, producing tens of thousands of prints and lantern slides, and several photographic albums, chief among them being the splendid five-volume publication containing 191 large (0.23 x 0.28 m.) albumen prints: *Souvenirs d'Orient. Album pittoresque des sites, villes et ruines les plus remarquables . . .* (vol. 1 & 2:) *de l'Egypte et de la Nubie,* (vol. 3:) *de la Terre-Sainte,* (vol. 4:) *de la Syrie et de la Côte d'Asie,* (vol. 5): *d'Athènes et Constantinople, avec notice historique, archéologique et descriptive en regard de chaque planche.* Photographié et edité par Félix Bonfils, auteur et éditeur des voyages d'Egypte, de Syrie, de Grèce et de Constantinople. Chez l'auteur, à Alais (Gard), 1877-78.

The Bonfils studio also excelled in portrait photography, group and ethnic studies, and scenes of craftsmen at work, and produced more photographs of people of the Middle East than perhaps any other studio of its time, including many shots of female subjects credited to Lydie Bonfils. However, it is dubious whether many of the portrait and ethnic studies can be used as an accurate guide to the dress or social conventions of the time, since a good number were taken in studios using paid sitters artfully arranged against painted backdrops and studio props. The aim in taking many of these photographs was not to duplicate reality authentically, but to create picturesque scenes.

La Maison Bonfils maintained studios in Beirut and Alais (now Alès), France but as the volume of work expanded and the demand for photographs increased, regional branches were established in Jerusalem, Baalbek, Alexandria, and Cairo. With the death of Félix Bonfils in 1885, management of the firm passed to his son, Adrien, who had been active in the business since 1878. He kept up the enormous output of the studio and photographed extensively in the Middle East until 1895 when he abandoned the business to open up a hotel in the town of Brummāna, located in the mountains overlooking Beirut. By the 1890s the Kodak box camera, invented by George Eastman in 1888, was in such widespread use that the professional studies had become obsolete. Lydie Bonfils maintained the studio in Beirut and continued to photograph until evacuated from Beirut by the United States Navy in 1916. Abraham Guiragossian, an Armenian photographer from Palestine, took over the Beirut studio and continued to reproduce nineteenth century Bonfils negatives until the eve of the Second World War. However, he discarded many of the original negatives, doubtless to make room for other photographic equipment in the studio, and when he finally closed shop, the remainder were most likely destroyed. Michel Ecochard, the French architect and city planner, purchased 18 original Bonfils glass negatives from a street seller in Beirut during the 1930s for the price of the glass. Negatives of other photographers suffered a similar fate. Those of Tancrède Dumas were reused as panes for a greenhouse, while other studios simply destroyed their old negatives. But deliberate destruction can also lead to some amazing discoveries. In 1970 a bomb blast directed at the offices of the Center for International Affairs, located above the Harvard Semitic Museum in Cambridge, blew off the roof of the building. Scores of boxes, containing some 28,000 photographic images of the Middle East preserved in almost perfect condition, were revealed under the attic eaves. Since this discovery, the curator of the Museum, Carney E. S. Gavin, and his staff have been involved in an extensive project to assemble a comprehensive archive of nineteenth century photography of the Middle East and to make their research and photographic collection available to the public and scholars of many fields for which these photographs provide invaluable documentation. Most of the photographs in the Harvard Semitic Museum collection were produced by the Bonfils studio, and it is to Carney Gavin and his staff that we owe the major research on the history of this most prolific photographic firm and the recent interest generated in the early photography of the Middle East. The complete Harvard Semitic Museum collection of Bonfils photographs is now being prepared for publication in textfiche format by the University of Chicago Press.

108. *Alexandrie des Consuls*
[Alexandria. Formerly Place des Consuls and more recently Place Muḥammad ʿAlī, now known as Liberation Square. The equestrian statue of Muḥammad ʿAlī by the French sculptor A. Jacquemart stands in the center of the square]
(10)   0.223 x 0.285   Bonfils ca. 1875-82
Collection Blackburn

109. *Sphynx et pyramide*
[The Sphinx and Pyramid of Cheops at Giza]
(394)   0.272 x 0.335   ca. 1870s
Collection Blackburn

110. *Damas, Porte de la rue droite ou de*
Bab-Charki (Syrie)
[Damascus, East Gate of the City (Bāb Sharqī)]
(185)   Bonfils ca. 1870
Studio Dorka, Paris

111. *Damas, Porte de la rue Droite ou de Bab-Charki*

[Damascus, East Gate of the city (Bāb Sharqī)]
(416)   0.239 x 0.304   Bonfils ca. 1880s
Collection Ecochard, Paris

112. *Damas, Grande mosquée et vue générale de Damas*
[Damascus, the Umayyad Mosque built by the Caliph al-Walīd between 706 and 715. The view is taken from atop the southwest minaret of the mosque looking northeast, showing the northern colonnade and northern minaret of the mosque, known as the Minaret of the Bride]
(784)   0.239 x 0.304   Bonfils ca. 1880s
Collection Ecochard, Paris

113. *Source de Ain Fidjeh*
[The spring of ʿAyn al-Fija, the chief source of the Baradā River, which supplies water to Damascus]
(380)   0.239 x 0.307   Bonfils ca. 1880s
Collection Ecochard, Paris

112.   Damascus, the Umayyad Mosque and general view of the city looking northeast
(Adrien Bonfils, ca. 1880s) Collection Ecochard, Paris

G. ZANGAKI

G. Zangaki, a photographer probably of Greek origin, established a studio in Port Saʿīd at the entrance to the Suez Canal, and produced a substantial volume of photographs throughout the 1870s and 1880s. The photographs of Zangaki in the Department of Special Collections are mounted in a tourists' album compiled by an English or an American traveler on a tour through France, Egypt, Greece, and Italy in 1898-99. The album contains 121 photographs of France, 62 of Egypt, 24 of Greece, and 12 of Italy, and most of the mounts are inscribed with the date on which the site recorded in the photograph was visited. The earliest entry date is June 2, 1898, and the latest is March 17, 1899. Of the 62 photographs of Egypt, the earliest date recorded is November 15, 1898, and the latest, January 28, 1899. Thirty-nine of the photographs of Egypt are signed by Zangaki, 11 by A. Beato, and 12 have no mark of authorship. All of these photographs are albumen prints and appear to have been taken in the 1880s.

Just as the modern traveler takes snapshots on tours abroad to record the sights in each country visited, the nineteenth century traveler collected photographic prints from studios in each country which he later pasted into an album as a memento of the trip. This provided photographers with a brisk business until the appearance of the Kodak box camera which made photography available to the masses and put many of the professionals out of work.

Tourists' Album [1898-99]
219 mounted photographs of France (nos. 1-121), Egypt (nos. 122-183), Greece (nos. 184-207), and Italy (nos. 208-219)

Volume: 0.239 x 0.335 m
Image: ca. 0.218 x 0.28 m

114. *Panorama de vieux Caire et pyramides*

[Panorama of Cairo and the Pyramids taken from the Citadel]
123 (296)   0.217 x 0.283   Zangaki

115. *Caire, Panorama de la Citadelle*
[Cairo, view of the eastern side of the Citadel taken from the Maqaṭṭam Hills]
124 (295)   0.218 x 0.273   Zangaki

115. Cairo, view of the eastern side of the Citadel and the Mosque of Muḥammad ʿAlī (1848) taken from the Muqaṭṭam Hills (Zangaki, ca. 1880s)

Mrs. Isabella Lucy Bird Bishop (1831-1904) is described in her obituary in the *New York Times* of October 8, 1904, as "one of the most daring women travelers who ever lived." She was born in Yorkshire, England on October 15, 1831, and began her travels at the age of twenty-two. Her numerous books of travel record the many areas of the globe which she covered. Among the books which she wrote are: *The English Woman in America*; *The Hawaiian Archipelago, Six Months among the Palm Groves, Coral Reefs and Volcanoes of the Sandwich Islands*; *A Lady's Life in the Rocky Mountains*; *Unbeaten Tracks in Japan, an Account of the Travel in the Interior Including Visits to the Aborigines of Yezo and Shrines of Nikko and Isé*; *The Golden Chersonese and the Way Thither*; *The Yangtze Valley and Beyond, an Account of Journeys in China, chiefly in the Province of Sze Chuan and among the Man-tze of the Somo Territory*; *Chinese Pictures, Notes on Photographs Made in China*; *Among the Tibetans*; and *Korea and Her Neighbors, a Narrative of Travel, with an Account of the Recent Vicissitudes and Present Position of the Country*.

She was connected with philanthropic work of various forms, especially in the medical mission field, and built five hospitals and an orphan asylum in the Far East. She was the first woman to be elected a Fellow of the Royal Geographical Society, and was also an honorary member of the Oriental Society of Peking.

During 1890 she spent nine months in Persia. She began her trip at Basra, sailed to Baghdad, traveled overland to western Iran where she spent most of her time amongst the Bakhtiari nomads, then continued northwestward through eastern Turkey, and ended her trip at Trabzon on the Black Sea. An account of her journey was published in two volumes, *Journeys in Persia and Kurdistan, Including a Summer in the Upper Karun Region and a Visit to the Nestorian Rayahs* (New York: G. P. Putnam's Sons, 1891), and an album of 101 photographs taken by Mrs. Bishop on this trip, interleaved with her own descriptive text, was also published under the title, *I. B.* [Isabella Bird] *Photographs Persia 1890*. A selection of these photographs is exhibited with portions of the descriptive text which accompany each photograph.

116. Iran, the Shamsabad defile and bridge viewed from its northern entrance (Bishop, 1890)

BISHOP, ISABELLA LUCY (BIRD)

I. B. [Isabella Bird] *Photographs Persia 1890*
n.p., n.d. [1891]

101 mounted photographs interleaved with descriptive text. The photographs are numbered 1-156; nos. 43 and 144 are missing and nos. 31, 32, 39-42, 58-79, 82, 83, 85, 88, 96, 99, 106-09, 111, 112, 122, 125, 131, 136, 138-43, 147, 149 and 151 are not included.
Volume: 0.303 x 0.412 m
Image: ca. 0.155 x 0.209 m

116. *The Shamsabad defile and bridge viewed from its northern entrance*
6   0.156 x 0.209

117. *A group in the (Christian) Armenian village near Gundaman. The houses are of sun-dried brick, and the village shows signs of prosperity, though many poorly-clad are seen. The Bakhtiari scull group is worn as a sign of being under Bakhtiari protection. The village has a couple of Armenian priests and a church, though without any outward sign of being one. The white cloth worn by the women is a general Armenian custom to denote subjection and the silence imposed on the sex by the church. Of course it is merely a matter of form, and the civilizing influence imparted by the schools in Julfa is confining this hideous custom to the elder women.*
12   0.157 x 0.21

118. *A group of women and children on the weekly holiday outing to the shrine of Gandaman. The shrine is hidden by the foliage at the back of the group. They are Deh-nishin (settled down) Bakhtiaris intermarried with Persian women. Unacquainted with a camera, they suddenly become shy, and showed signs of fright on the photographer's head disappearing below the focusing cloth. No honeyed words nor promises of money could bring them back to the brink of the stream flowing out of the rock only 30 yards distant, in which they were at first seen playing with the children amidst happy laughter, screams, and romps. With intelligent, if not pretty faces, large long eyes, sturdy physique, and a sharp tongue, the women of even these more Persian parts retain some of the freedom inherited from their Bakhtiari sisters.*
15   0.156 x 0.209

119. *Types of the Bakhtiari Lur, the living and the dead. The living on his well protected and much cherished hardy mare is on his way to his home near the village in the distance. He is silent and short spoken. A well featured, well set up hardy mounted mountaineer, a cartridge belt around his waist, with a dagger and pistol in his kamar-band, a "Martina" (Martini Peabody) invariably slung over his shoulder, a sword under his saddle flaps, with its handle, as it should be,*

always handy, just in front of his left thigh; with the eye of a hawk, and a heart of oak, he is one of a few thousand it makes one's mouth water to train and command. He is by birth a soldier, modest, yet with proper self-esteem. He is fully aware of his deficiencies and of the failings of his race, but he rightly attributes them to be the outcome of external and unsought for conditions. He is a Theist, and believing in Revelation has elevated aspirations. A Mussulman by heredity, he in his heart rails and scoffs at Mullah and Sayad. His country possesses no mosque or religious building beyond the dilapidated shrine of some departed saint. He is open to good influence, and likes to hear of noble deeds of self-sacrifice.

In imitation of the living, the dead Lur's tomb, always a rough hewn lion, invariably carries the sword, the musket, the dagger, the pouch, and the cartridge belt. The graveyards, generally on low mounds, are unprotected by fence or wall.
16   0.157 x 0.21

120 *A "black tent" family group. The chief lady and wife in the centre. The other members of the family and servants in attendance. The lord and master is absent in attendance of his chief. A deaf boy, one of the sons, is in a miseri-cordium attitude to the right. The eldest boy to the left is in charge.*

The dwellers in "black tents" have no privacy, and living thus all the year round might justify the presumption of a low standard of domestic virtue; but such is not the case; on the contrary, the matrimonial ties (even if numerous) are faithfully and strictly kept, children are highly esteemed and much loved, and domestic happiness would seem the rule even among the poorest. The ruling vice of the Persian and the Afghan is unknown.
18   0.156 x 0.209

121. *A type of a Bakhtiari gentleman. Lutf Ali Khan is a large landed proprietor in the Sabz Kuh Valley. A nephew of Isfandiar Khan, he is his great partisan. A keen sportsman, and a well-mannered man of 30; he is all that could be desired as a future leader, with whom it would be a pleasure to have official connection. . . . A splendid horseman, he has his stable full of good, light, well-blooded horses. He is an excellent shot.*
23   0.156 x 0.207

122. *A group at Ardal. The Ilbegi (literally 2nd-in-command of the Bakhtiaris), Isfandiar Khan, son of the late Ilkhani (chief), Hussein Kulli Khan, who was treacherously arrested and killed by the Zil, was arrested at the time of his father's death, and for six years after wore prisoner's chains. He is now Samsam-ul-Sultaneh (the Sword of the Empire), and is seen*

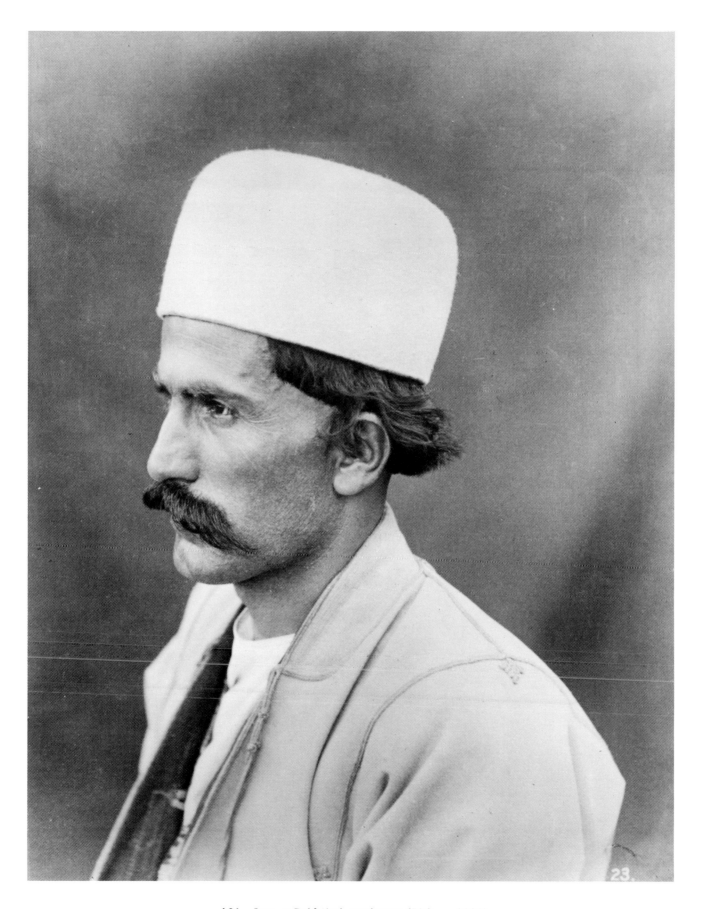

121. Iran, a Bakhtiari gentleman (Bishop, 1890)

seated in the chair surrounded by his nephews. The three standing behind are manly fellows, well armed, and extremely anxious to be considered civilized. Of the three little ones, the one on the left is deaf and dumb. The open hand striking the breast is a recognized attitude in these parts demanding human and divine commisseration.

28   0.152 x 0.206

123. *View of the northern end of the Zard Kuh taken from a spur of the Kuh-i-Rang from near the Gal-i-gav Pass, showing the Haft Tanan, the head-waters of the Kurang, and the commencement of the Pambakal Pass. The sharp Haft Tanan Peak has an estimated elevation of 13,000 feet.*

36   0.157 x 0.182

124. *A group of Bakhtiari women. The chief wife of majestic dimensions and full of fun. The youngest and newest wife in the center of the picture is determined to take her proper place away from among the more mercurial children. The iron cooking pot is characteristic; it has a useful and yet artistic design.*

45   0.157 x 0.209

125. *A group of Bakhtiaris taken near Ardal. The Haji Ilkhani and his brother Reza Kulli Khan are seated in Feringi chairs, there being none of these articles in the whole Bakhtiari country. The rifle is a Peabody Martini with silver bands added. The Bakhtiaris are fair shots at distances under 400 yards. Firing at greater distances is to them waste of ammunition.*

46   0.153 x 0.207

126. *Yahia Khan, chief of the Mian Kuh tribe of the Pulandwand section of the Chhar Lang Bakhtiaris. Standing 6 feet 2 inches, weighing 16 stone, he is a fierce looking man, of great ability, exceedingly civil and obliging, protesting great admiration for all Englishmen and their Queen. At present in great distress at the exhorbitant demands made upon him by the Persian authorities. . . . He suffers from having too many wives, some young and pretty, but for all that is active, robust, and longing for the day when _____. His country is a nice country, with wooded hills and meadow valleys, inhabited all the year round.*

80   0.157 x 0.197

127. *A group of Bakhtiaris in the Upper Kurang*

84   0.157 x 0.209

128. *A group of Zalaki women. The central figures being the chief ladies in their Sunday best. The favourite color is dark indigo—almost black. They wear the divided skirt, a handsome light chemisette, and over all a dark-coloured linen sheet, which, after covering the breast and shoulders, is carried on to the head, forming a kind of turban.* The tout ensemble *is striking, becoming, and practical for the lives they lead. The women all possess handsome features, and frequently are blessed with a soft expression; but as a rule their faces have a* noli me tangere *and severe look, inculcating the utmost respect, even from their own lords and masters, who generally are said to treat their wives with perfect equality. The children are treated affectionately and well in all respects. The girls of the well-to-do on reaching maturity are said to have the right to veto their parents' choice of a husband—a kind "of selection based upon rejection" system, which may be a step towards the more civilized and modern system of "selection based on favouritism."*

102   0.155 x 0.206

129. *The large alcove of the Tak-i-Bostan. The owner's son and a party of Kurd visitors, and the authoress Isabella Bird in the foreground.*

124   0.154 x 0.212

130. *A group of Armenian women and girls attending the C.M.S. Mission School. With the unmixed race blood of centuries running through their veins, they seem mostly cast in the same mould. Large liquid eyes, a fair skin with sometimes a ruddy hue, with a gentle, soft, graceful manner, they are frequently admired.*

    The hideous plan of covering the mouth is said to be a time honored custom as a mark of respect towards the lord and master, and an outward sign to the woman to keep silent in his presence! This custom is said to be fast disappearing as being unsanitary, meaningless, and undesirable.

152   0.157 x 0.211

131. *Types of Persian Cavalry stationed at Isfahan under the command of the "Mir Panj." The coats are blue grey, of Russian pattern. The cap is white lambswool.*

155   0.157 x 0.177

122. Iran, a group at Ardal (Bishop, 1890)

GULMEZ FRÈRES

Gulmez Frères, a photographic studio established in Istanbul, was active during the latter part of the nineteenth century. An album produced by this studio is in the collection of Dr. Ralph Jaeckel. The cover of this album displays the tughra (signature) of the Ottoman Sultan, Abdul-Hamid II (1876-1909). Below the tughra is the title of the album, *Constantinople*, and on the lower right-hand corner is the name of the photographic firm which produced this album, Gulmez Frères. On the first page of the album is written a dedication:

Hommage de respectueuse admiration
A. L. E. Mikael Effendi Portocal

Below the dedication on the right-hand corner of the page is the name of the photographic firm, Gulmez Frères, and underneath, the place and date: Constantinople, le 1re Janvier 1893. The album contains 40 mounted photographic prints which all appear to date from the 1880s or early 1890s. Thirty-six of these prints are of monuments and scenic sights in and around Istanbul, including fifteen of the Church of the Monastery of the Chora (known as the Kariye Camii), splendidly decorated with mosaics and frescoes dating from the fourteenth century, and four of the prints are views of Bursa. Practically all of the prints are numbered, identified, and signed "Gulmez Frères." Fourteen of the fifteen photographs of the Kariye Camii are shots of the mosaics covering the interior of the church. These are the first known photographs to have been taken of these beautiful mosaics, and the quality of reproduction compares favorably with the more recently published photographs of these mosaics found in the second and third volumes of Paul A. Underwood's impressive study, *The Kariye Djami* (3 vols. New York: Bollingen Foundation, 1966).

132. Istanbul, view of the Galata Bridge spanning the Golden Horn
(Gulmez Frères, ca. 1890) Collection Ralph Jaeckel

GULMEZ FRÈRES
Constantinople
n.p., n.d. [1893]

40 mounted photographic prints
Volume: 0.307 x 0.40 m
Image: 0.215 x 0.268 m
Collection Ralph Jaeckel

132. *Le Pont de Karakeuy*
[Istanbul, view of the Galata Bridge spanning the Golden Horn with Galata (Karaköy) and Pera (Beyoğlu) on the other side. The Galata Tower, built by the Genoese in 1348, commands the summit of the former Genoese colony of Pera]
(52)   0.215 x 0.268   Gulmez Frères

After Daguerre: Masterworks of French Photography (1848-1900) from the Bibliothèque Nationale. Exhibition catalog. New York: The Metropolitan Museum of Art, in association with Berger-Levrault, Paris, 1980.

Arts Council of Great Britain. *'From Today Painting is Dead', The Beginnings of Photography.* Exhibition Catalog. London: Shenval, 1972.

Baier, Wolfgang. *Quellendarstellungen zur Geschichte der Fotografie.* Munich: Schirmer/Mosel, 1977.

Bonfils, Félix. *Catalogue des vues photographiques de l'Orient, photographiées et editées par Bonfils Félix.* Alais: A. Brugueirolle et Compagnie, 1876.

Bull, Deborah and Lorimer, Donald. *Up the Nile, a Photographic Excursion: Egypt 1839-1898.* New York: Potter, 1979.

Carella, Elizabeth. "Bonfils and his Curious Composite." *Exposure* 17 (Spring 1979): 26-33.

Chevedden, Paul E. "Bonfils & Son, Egypt, Greece and the Levant—Correspondence." *History of Photography* 5 (January 1981): 82.

Coke, Van Deren. *Nineteenth Century Photographs from the Collection, Art Museum, University of New Mexico.* Exhibition Catalog. Albuquerque: University Art Museum, University of New Mexico, 1976.

Collins, Lydia. "Nineteenth Century Photographs in the Palestine Exploration Fund Collection." *Palestine Exploration Quarterly* 113 (January-June 1981): 63-66.

Eldem, Sedad Hakkı. *Boğaziçi Anıları (Reminiscences of the Bosphorus).* Istanbul: Aletaş Alarko Eğitim Tesisleri A.Ş., 1979.

Eldem, Sedad Hakkı. *Istanbul Anıları (Reminiscences of Istanbul).* Istanbul: Aletaş Alarko Eğitim Tesisleri A.Ş., 1979.

Frith, Francis. *Comparative Photography: A Century of Change in Egypt and Israel.* Photographs by Francis Frith and Jane Reese Williams; intro. by Brian W. Fagan. Carmel, Calif.: Friends of Photography, 1979.

Frith, Francis. *Egypt and the Holy Land in Historic Photographs, 77 Views by Francis Frith.* Introduction by J. Van Haaften, selection and commentary by J.E.M. White. New York: Dover, 1980.

Galassi, Peter. *Before Photography, Painting and the Invention of Photography.* New York: Museum of Modern Art, 1981.

Gautier-van Berchem, Marguerite and Ory, Solange. *La Jérusalem Musulmane dans l'oeuvre de Max van Berchem.* Lausanne: Editions des Trois Continents, 1978.

Gavin, Carney E. S. "Bonfils and the Early Photography of the Near East," *Harvard Library Bulletin* 26 (October 1978): 442-70.

Gavin, Carney E. S. "History's Invisible Treasures: Early Mideastern Photos." *Jordan* 5 (Summer 1980): 12-15.

Gavin, Carney E. S. "The Work of the Photographers Bonfils, 1867-1916." *Nineteenth Century* 6 (Winter 1980): 42-47.

Gavin, E. S.; Carella, E.; and O'Reilly, I. "The Photographers Bonfils of Beirut and Alès, 1867-1916." *Camera* 60 (March 1981): 4-36.

Goldschmidt, Lucien and Naef, Weston J. *The Truthful Lens: A Survey of the Photographically Illustrated Book, 1844-1914.* New York: Grolier Club, 1980.

Graham-Brown, Sarah. *Palestinians and Their Society, 1880-1946; a Photographic Essay.* London: Quartet Books, 1980.

Henisch, B. A. and H. K. "Robertson of Constantinople," *Image* 17, no. 3 (1974): 1-9.

Henisch, B. A. and H. K. "Souvenir de Constantinople." *History of Photography* 4 (July 1980): 205-06.

Hill, Stephen. *Gertrude Bell (1868-1926), a Selection from the Photographic Archive of an Archaeologist and Traveller.* Newcastle upon Tyne: The University, 1977.

Hobart, George S. "The Matson Collection: A Half Century of Photography in the Middle East." *The Quarterly Journal of the Library of Congress* 30 (January 1973): 19-43.

Jammes, André and Jammes, Marie-Thérèse. "Egypt in Flaubert's Time: the First Photographers, 1839-1860." *Aperture* 78 (1977): 62-77.

Jammes, Isabelle. "Louis-Désiré Blanquart-Evrard, 1802-1872," *Camera* 57 (December 1978): 3-44.

Jay, Bill. *Victorian Cameraman; Francis Frith's Views of Rural England, 1850-1898.* Newton Abbot: David & Charles, 1973.

Landau, Jacob M. *Abdul-Hamid's Palestine.* London: Andre Deutsch, 1979.

Matson, G. Eric. *The Middle East in Pictures, a Photographic History, 1898-1934.* 4 vols. New York: Arno Press, 1980.

Merrill, Selah. "List of Photographic Views, taken expressly for the American Palestine Exploration Society, during a Reconnoissance East of the Jordan, in the Autumn of 1875." *Palestine Exploration Society Statement* 4 (January 1877): 101-13.

Nassau, William E. "Treasures on Glass and Celluloid: Conservation Work on the Photographic Archives of the Palestine Exploration Fund." *Palestine Exploration Quarterly* 110 (July-December 1978): 131-133.

"Notes and News." *Palestine Exploration Quarterly* 110 (July-December 1978): 73-74.

Onne, Eyal. *Photographic Heritage of the Holy Land, 1839-1914.* Manchester: Manchester Polytechnic, 1980.

Ory, Solange. *Archives Max van Berchem. Conservées à la Bibliothèque Publique et Universitaire de Genève. Catalogue de la Photothèque.* Leiden: Brill, 1975.

Palestine Exploration Fund. *Catalogue of Photographic Views illustrating Old and New Testament Sites, Monuments and Objects of Interest, and Manners and Customs.* London: Guildford, Billing and Sons, 1892.

Piemontese, Angelo M. "The Photograph Album of the Italian Diplomatic Mission to Persia (Summer 1862)." *East and West*, n.s., 22 (September-December 1972): 249-311.

Scarce, Jennifer. *Isfahan in Camera: 19th Century Persia through the Photographs of Ernst Hoeltzer.* London: Art and Archaeology Research Papers, 1976.

Schaaf, Larry: "Charles Piazzi Smyth's 1865 Conquest of the Great Pyramid," *History of Photography* 3 (October 1979): 331-54.

Schiller, Ely (ed.) *The First Photographs of Jerusalem.* Jerusalem: Ariel Publishing Co., 1978. (Vol. 1, *The Old City*; Vol. 2, *The New City*.)

Sobieszek, Robert A. "La Maison Bonfils." *American Photographer* (November, 1980): 48-57.

Sobieszek, Robert A. and Gavin, Carney E. S. *Remembrances of the Near East; The Photographs of Bonfils, 1867-1907.* Exhibition Catalog. Rochester, N.Y.: International Museum of Photography at George Eastman Home, 1980.

Steegmuller, Francis (éd.) *Flaubert in Egypt: A Sensibility on Tour.* Boston & Toronto: Little Brown & Co., 1972.

Tassel, Janet Q. "Dragomans, Sheiks and Moon-Faced Beauties." *Art News* (December 1980): 106-109.

Thomas, Ritchie. "The Tin-Box Photos." *ARAMCO World Magazine* 26 (September-October 1975): 26-32.

Thomas, Ritchie. "Bonfils & Son, Egypt, Greece and the Levant; 1867-1894." *History of Photography* 3 (January 1979): 33-46.

Thomas, Ritchie. "Some 19th Century Photographers in Syria, Palestine and Egypt." *History of Photography* 3 (April 1979): 157-166.

Upton, Joseph M. *Catalogue of the Herzfeld Archive.* Washington, D.C.: Freer Gallery of Art, 1978.

Van Haaften, Julia. " 'Original Sun Pictures,' a Check List of the New York Public Library's Holdings of Early Works Illustrated with Photographs, 1844-1900." *Bulletin of the New York Public Library* 80 (Spring 1977): 355-415.

Weinberg, Adam D. *Majestic Inspirations, Incomparable Souvenirs; Nineteenth Century Photographs of the Mediterranean and the Middle East from the Collection of Brandeis University.* Exhibition Catalog. Waltham, Mass.: Rose Art Museum, Brandeis University, 1977.

The great difficulty in Photography is to get the Sitter to assume a Pleasing Expression of Countenance—Jones, however, thinks that, in this instance, he has been extremely successful.

Punch, June 7, 1862, p. 230. The photographer identified under the pseudonym of "Jones" in this cartoon is actually Francis Frith shown with the same beard and fez as in his photograph on p. iv (no. 13). This cartoon attests to the notoriety Frith achieved in England with his photographs of the Middle East.